Influence of Place

Ernestine Louise

Influence of Place

[Poems]

The Writers
Book Project Press

The Writers Book Project Press

First printing September 2019

Cover Photograph by Ernestine Louise

Cover Design & back cover photograph by Stig Marlon Weston

Book Design by Ernestine Louise & K. J. Wright

Names: Ernestine Louise, 1972- author

Title: Influence of Place / Ernestine Louise

Description: Oslo, Norway : The Writers Book Project Press, 2019

Identifiers: ISBN 978-82-691659-0-6

www.ernestinelouise.com

For the dreams that fuel the desire to create
and the belief in yourself to do it.

In loving memory of Brandon.

And for my mother –
something from nothing

Contents

[II]

Influence of Place

Preface

Influence of Place is my journey into the places around me,
inside of me, and the ones that I do not realize actually exist
until I begin to write. I am intrigued by how place manifests
itsclf in what I create. This collection of poetry is an
exploration of the impact that place has on me as a writer.

Place impacts directly/indirectly, from past to present, the
experiences that shape how the telling occurs. It is the idea
that place, as an experience, is not only that of the physical
environment, but also the nonphysical environment. Place in
its tangible and intangible ways has been a wonderful muse.
It has been exciting to view place from its perspective
and how it shares its story.

Art is also a major influence on my writing. Modernism and
abstract art in particular. I am interested in the complexities
of these two styles and how they shape my poetry and prose.
Poetry lends itself more willingly to exploring these mediums,
which can be more challenging in my opinion to do with
words. And I am also aware that these complexities can also
prevent the reader or observer from understanding what or how
they are and can engage.

I do not try to avoid this tension in these pages. The page is my canvas and words are my paint. This can be seen in the way that I place the words on the page as well as the length of some of the poems. I want the reader to bring their personal experiences, ideas, bias, thoughts, and perspectives to reading *Influence of Place*. You may love a poem, be unsure about its meaning, or just scratch your head. I welcome all of these experiences and interpretations.

I have questions that I constantly ask myself when I am engaged in the writing process. How can language be used to color inside or outside the lines? How does language leave space for interpretation and exploration by the reader? What lines connect or disconnect the viewer to the narrative? Allowing myself to be open to how *Influence of Place* could be written has challenged my way of thinking of writing and it has been fun.

Thank you for joining me on this journey. I hope that you find something in these pages, whatever that may be. Please share your own journey with *Influence of Place* at www.ernestinelouise.com.

The best of everything wonderful and positive,

Ernestine Louise

[I]

Opening

small world wrapped in/end less ness/ invisible/cracks/draw
   in/closer/freedom/open/smile/a little/

each laugh hides shards of loss/a coming of age story/
   less train wreck/more guided tour/

shapeless and unformed ideas/move on a canvas/
   perfect imperfections/ hope/love/normal/you are all of these/
while i am none/

angels/from the brink of nothingness/before it is understood/
   appear/the right time/the right place/move/begin anew/
framed by past memories/

light/a glimpse of the world/as it should exist/
   sits at the edge/in the direction of me/opening

The Process

Write a poem   like it just jumps onto pages out of air
        What is accomplished   if there is no action
time makes it possible

Don't waste the moments   not many people have
        the opportunities to do

A process left to discovering the truths   faults
        the language beauty unfolds

Walk don't walk   just write something
        you need to work

Each breath is a word   sometimes a whole book
     about a butterfly opening

Sleep brings something new   disruptive flow a break
     in between long gazes

A walk through the park   overheard meaningless
     silly conversations   turn into words

Finding place on pages   is not like setting
     dinner tables with placards

Input impedes the output   sorting through the trash
     finding gems takes time

Photographers aren't told   take the shot
    they think   test   make images

Producing something to feel   accomplished at
    the end   it's not needle work

Stitching together is not weaving language into
    thought   Keyboard taps aren't joy

Think   write   edit
    think   write   doubt   question   edit
                    each blink   is writing

Art Imitates Life

The Aragonese alabaster was used in a torrent of creative
expression and marvelous wonders on display.

I often wonder about the what ifs in life
What if I were a man
the world would be my oyster
But then I realize that I am the world
so what ifs don't matter
the art of my existence does

Lyrics of History Repeat

1

Seventeen-Twenty-six.
Uninformed impressions.
A memory.
Not good.
Not bad.

Memory.
Worth remembering.
Forgetting.
Small details.
Recalling.
Most important.

Touch words.
Feel connected.
Time and space.

Name unknown.
Without knowing intentions.
Take advice.

Trust you.
To show something unknown.
And I don't know your name.

2

Walking backwards from now.
I know your name.
You know my name.

Trust less.
Time and space.
Connect us.

Strangers.
Aware.
Living breeds.
Inevitable familiarity.

In you me.
Seek again.
Each other.
Find.

Home.
Abandonment.
Wrapped memories.
Outline frame.
Life inhabit.

Seek freedom.
Seek self.
In good.
In bad.
Seek us.

Seventeen-twenty-six.
Believe.
Doubts.

3

Memories past.
Face present.
Avoid future.

Existing requires.
A plan.
To there.

A moment.
Now filled.
Memories past.
Future thoughts.

Smile.
Leave speechless.
Fooling.
You.
Her.
Not me.
Fall into.

4

Empty.
Full.
True.
Deliverance.
Worshipped.

Swept.
Away.
Reality.
Broken.
Lyrics on repeat.

Voice raised.
Music hums.
Catch an experience in a song.
Personal interpretation.
Disconnects shared memory.

Warning signs.
You can never go back.
Moving forward.
Watch yourself made pitfalls.

Time will tell.
If you enjoyed life.
Smile the same way.

5

Memories shape.
Darkness.
Richness.
Deepness.
Newness.

Look for the wonderful life.
In the wonder of living it fully.
Explain less.
Experience more.

Seventeen-twenty-six equals forty-three.
Age of past knowing.
Present.
Future.

6

Watch you.
Walk out.
Thought.
Here we are again.
Memory making.

Not bad.
Not good.
Lyrics of history repeat.

Dehydration

Reason's vessel.
Open space to fill.
Clear mind – empty.
Logic has no tempo.
Keep a step ahead.

          Hear something forbidden.
          Take a step back.
          Guide me.
          You're needed sometimes.
          Not to be everything.
          To be that thing.
          Free.

                    Into.
                    Deep kiss.
                    Deep kiss.
                    Deep kiss.

Until you cannot be.
Walk to the mountain top.
Take a deep breath.
And transfer it.

Mindful desire.
A place.
Traversing.
Vast.
Possible.
Moments.

Stranded in your desert.
Water sits just in sight.
But you're too lazy.
To reach for it.

The Light That Frames

The light that frames the mountains rises from the east.
Everything rises from the east.
Something to do with gravitational pull or the
Earth's rotation on an axis.
The explanation for why it does was clear
before I started this poem,
but then I realized that it doesn't matter.
What really matters is that
the light that frames the mountains rises from the east.
It's important because it was the
direction that I was moving in, not by foot, but by memory.
Little big things cover the larger things
that look so far away. Now facing downward
everything seems smaller from the top
and the top seems infinite even when blocked
by cloudy blue sky, star studded
darkness or pitch blackness. Breaking through - beyond
the troposphere isn't easier, even when
the light that frames the mountains rises in the east.
Tracing steps found on a trail left by
animals trampled over by eager trail runners.

You know the type who stop to pee at the summit, take a
quick selfie and immediately turn around to
head back down – rather than enjoy the accomplishment of
making it to turning around to see the panoramic
view providing a different perspective. A lost moment of
self reflection?
Perhaps self reflection happens while relieving the bladder.
More water required.

Rock Forms Me

Follow me through the wooded places that turn into desert,
        jungle and forest;
Follow me into the canyon's dry riverbeds watched over by
        giants willingly trapped in pebbles and stone;
Follow me formed into a magic mountain that is full of cruel
                grace;
Follow me placed where creating something with someone
        who should not exist and who will not exist is fair game.

Follow me break open into a trillion particle pieces as a
        reminder that everything is everything because it is
                nothing;
Follow me returned effulgent - a star, planet to touch,
        live on with but cannot reach;
Follow me pretend to understand even though it is impossible to
                understand;
Follow me everything and yet nothing allowed to exist in this
                moment;
Follow me disappear into black hole comet and meteor consume
        each peak climbed.

Follow me summit and canyon – ebb flow into shade
        from shadows living dead;

Follow me scratched and beaten by invisible hands throwing
     down rocks and rain;
Follow me into and out of the blue black sky caught on fire
     at sunset wrapping body and another body;
Follow me Goddess to godless searching the heavens
     above to find the soul beneath.

Follow me dark and light places recalling empty spaces
     filled with two forgetting thoughts of three.

Follow me seeing and wanting the top to be the bottom and
     the peak to be a valley ending and beginning;
Follow me transformed into rock effaced by fingers incapable
     of touch holding tightly memories never forgotten but
          never recalled;
Follow me trails disguised as witches and spells cast by cave
     hermits;
Follow me overlook mountain goat path leading to shear drops
     steep climb to sanctuary with spectacular views.

Follow me flesh and bone to elephant rocks holding history and
     secrets never to be shared or forgotten;
Follow me stand on the edge waiting for a push over free fall
     into freedom caught by rocks below;
Follow me heart pounds little steps to a beat no answers no
     calls no;
Follow me yes and it will be enough, it will be one step and
     then two;
Follow me to the place where rock forms me.

Watcher

Light   seeps   through   wood

    washing over
   sun
 lingers
at
 the last

     Losing sight
lightconnectstwoshadesofbluesky
    tracing bright multi-colors
             Peering
              out
       it's   time   to

            play

Sizing Up the World Around

Take notice of the wonder   the natural movements of nature
the teacher of fluidity and flow

Strangers things have I seen
        trees dancing to music of birds
mistaken solely for a windy day

A rat's appearance horrifies
        while cleaning up after its disgusting
host who invites it to eat their garbage

All the cultures of the world on the internet
        the world in a nutshell
leaves a divide greater than a seismic rift

The Things We See

The things you see when you look out of a window.

Bird shit drops from the sky   I assume that there is a bird
          either perched   above chatting away while relieving
itself   perhaps it could not pause   so it did it while in mid
          flight   I happened to catch sight of bird shit falling
when I looked out of the window

Watching two boys   either best friends
          first crush
          future best men
          or husbands
navigating their youth   creating memories   wasting time

Each day I see them through the window is a good day
          for me   in fact it's the best thing most days

I ad-lib their conversations in between the bites of their after-
               school snacks.
I marvel at the balance that they strike to accommodate each
          of their preferences for play   One stands   the other sits

They create a game   with an empty Pringles container
          that makes them laugh which in turn makes me smile
The story of their life in that moment   is told by me

I encroach on their playtime   I am not so vain to make
          their moments together my own   To them they are only
two   Me   the odd person out   and it's perfect

I am their invisible friend   who they don't know that they have
          or even need   my eyes find them when a I look out of
the window

          I never see the boys leave   it's a perfect end to our time
together   they together   and me   not wondering where they
               have gone

because their departure is not important
          but I look forward to their return

REM

Things that happen get stuck in memories   locked in a present
state of   illusion   fragmented in dreams.

Standing over on the edge   holding back arms   wings
fluttering   preparing to take flight   holding them still
to glance around the world.

Thrust movement through night   a mountain with the sea
below   waiting to catch whatever finds its way in
something   always   finds its way in   but never out
watching.

        Tracing the body's map of trauma
       roadblocks are surprises
        to know freedom   the past
            belongs to a set of mistakes
        leave open purpose   and cause to live.

A remnant of something similar to hope   a faint
red line
        that points to a small road that leads to the edge
                of water and stops
        waiting for a boat   to sail across.

A sepulcher crowded by low ceilings and tight seals   welcomes
home what little light can beat out air   the vastness in the dark
makes it all bigger than it is   with each breath   there is death
in life.

In the morning light interrupts REM   body moves   things that
were dormant are awake again   reliving a faint existence of joy
wrapped in a body laying still   full of grace.

        Remembering everything   happy to forget it all
        dark circles
                under blood red eyes   just another day   to put a best
                        foot
        forward   what was dead begins anew.

White

White bodies dressed in white clothes
        In the distance it looks normal

Sun beams, blue skies, sidewalks
        Full no one notices although everyone notices

White hanging from the edge
        It's clear confusion of what the brain communicates

And the eye sees
        Air blows white in the wind while

Strangers eat lunch and taxi
        Cabs wait hands grip bodies dangle

Light on the river makes the
        Bed more translucent rocks are below

It is not deep wading across
        With the ducks it's possible to enjoy

A reflection of white cloth dangles just above
        A black horse storms across and lifts it

The mouth opens wide white for the body
        To be free while everybody watches

Tread Lightly

Wonder is what wandering brings to bear

Thoughts that make a journey that will never be taken

Walk into the light of what

Find traces of feeling

Touch nothing and be full

Tread lightly though

Waking up is never fun

Spring Is Peaking

Seeking in the company of trees a cool breeze nestles against
my body.
I walk forward to sit next to an open space, alone is the journey.

Feeling hunger, thought less, empty. Destroying the construct of
dismantling myself. Allows me to breathe out
piece by piece deafening bells of crowded experiences.

Spring is peaking, just a little.
White blossoms are sent ahead to investigate.
But only birds are around. It is not time.

They wait for the arrival of
the bees that will announce the
time to live again has come.

Joy

Soiled underpants seated next to the boats entry point.
A man must have left them there   a woman knows better
        than to   air her dirty laundry   no matter whose pants
they are.

        Light hearted in work   joy   there on the table wrapped
in a gift box encased by paper   should be saved for
        another use.

        Skip along the path to joy   touching the things that
tickle and smell sweet.   Smell the beautiful
        color attached   to rooted sticks in the ground.

        Make noise filled with joy and glee.   Tears are for the
moments   when happiness leaves.   It's never clear
        it's just certain   that for a moment   sadness   will replace
joy.

        Joy   caught on barbwire surrounding your organ heart.
Breath in   breath out.

[II]

The Upswing

There is something fun in the upswing.
Up down up down.
No push for momentum just feet pump air.
Chest extends out in,
carefree movement – voluntary involuntary.
It takes you up down back forth,
higher higher bars behind you sky above.

Up down the bar on your neck
takes you up down but mostly down.
The wonder is on the down swing
crescent fallen chest.
The upswing is no fun. It is a myth
disguised as forward motion.
Talked about as if it did not exist at all.

When the up and down are
strict movements and stars are
too far away to make out which
one is which. There is no upswing
in dreaming when dreams have
ceased going up because they are
trapped in the back motion of down.

35

Untitled 1

     I should shed a tear   and allow
the pain   that is invisible to others
to grip   and paralyze my movements
but I have work
     I should kneel down   doubled over
in invisible angst   that grips me
     but I know that I will   never get up again.
     Taking a deep breath   without it
getting stuck in my rib cage
is challenging   Shallow breaths
sustain my life   and even that hurts
     The shower is the only place
that the tears will come   and I cannot
bring myself to enter it   there is not enough
water to wash away the devastation.
     Of the days that I remember there are nights
that I long to forget   A normal drive   turned
into a sudden stop on the pavement in front
of the metro exit

A scream in disbelief – strangers stop to console the unknown
the unthinkable   nothing can prepare you for loss   no one knows
how they will react when death knocks and you are left

hyperventilating   no matter how much you think that you
planned for it
    An SMS announced that my brother had died   my mother
called speaking calmly   to tell me that her youngest son is dead

    I hang the phone up abruptly because it's real   I had lost
the son that was my brother   The child I had raised   because
that's what the older siblings do   be parents to their younger
siblings we raise the younger ones   because our parents have
raised the older ones and are tired

    There are moments when the space in between my
disbelief and memories allow me to remember everything   Where
I was when I received the call   Where I was going when
I said hello   and the words   your brother is dead   were stuffed
down my throat   and caused my ears to bleed

    How I had the peace of mind to quietly say pull over and
only then   completely lose my shit   is beyond me   Perhaps self
preservation kicked in to avoid a car accident   How my mother
had the courage to call each of her living children to give us
the news   are things   that I don't think about as memories   or as
a part of that day

The loss is where my memory starts
slowly I walk myself to a good memory   to a
place that is more joy   than hurt
It's there   in this fake state of bliss
that everything is okay
        Death had never meant much to me
Other than its inevitableness   that by taking
your first breath   you are drawing nearer
to your last
        Now I know   a pain that can never be
explained   Everyone learns that their first heart
break sucks   And that grief   has its fives stages
        But death is a kind of loss that   is
something altogether different
It lingers after you have gone through the grieving
process   A constant companion holding
hands with you   skirting around the
edges of your heart
        My mother's voice   a reminder   imprinted
into a memory of someone who you
loved   and the reality of their   absence will
not be forgotten.

Time Is a Fading Thought

My friends end up somewhere they don't want to be   but
pretend that they do   It's early morning and the weekend   so it's
cool.

Waking to the tick of a clock   But ignoring its significance
Wandering around oblivious   lacking perception of what lays
ahead   caring not   that time has passed   only realizing that
you're late   but for what   you are not quite sure

Time is a fading thought   one that you have lost track of

Erasing Memory

She loves me
        I know it especially when my name rolls
        off her tongue with ease forget that moment
        when she introduced another man to me as her
        husband

The ladies
        where I live see my pain they want to be my
        friend and help me through this difficult time
        – lonely – but I'm not ready

I'm lonely
        for the wife that I had angry at the woman
        occupying my wife's body leaving me to
        understand that Elvis has left the building

It feels
        like the center of my world
        remembers me every other call and we speak
        twice a day it's okay but what happens when

She forgets

> me completely what then how did the Buddha
> live in the present and avoid the future holding
> onto the now is difficult it hurts so badly to have
> memories

Of ourselves

> only in the past it's more important than
> the present because often we are not us there and
> the future is me alone and her gone

If she

> were wheelchair bound this would be
> a walk in the park physically having to manage
> is less challenging than the mental emotional
> obstacles

That makes

> me so damn angry and hurt it's like walking
> backwards towards time caught in between lucid
> moments and lazy forgetfulness how much
> longer before I'm erased

Completely by

> something out of either of our control in sickness
> and in health til death do us part vows committed
> in love and hope never expecting that it meant to
> love in absence

Of memory
> of who we are to one another or that another man
> could fill my shoes and I in order to honor and
> love her should let him make her happy in the
> moments when she

Remembers being
> in love with someone but doesn't know
> that someone is me the ladies where I live want
> to help me but I am not ready to forget her

The Stories We Can Tell

Tell me a story before I go to sleep, one of the long
 ones.
            Wrapping fingers around fingers,
                 not quite wringing them with enthusiasm
                      but still quite dramatic.

Tell me about the places that make people
and people make other
            people and animals are people or not
                 but they seem like they are people.

Tell me the story about how you are and why you are who
you are and who I will be one day.
            Let's travel together to those places and meet strangers
                 and familiar friends. Tell me a story about where
                      you belong that is real even if
                           it doesn't exist.

Barcelona Beautiful

it's been a dream
only visited with clicks
through magazines and blogs online

to experience physically
the streets that raised
inspired and killed gaudí

a square fit for a king
trampled underfoot by foreigners
who want what's cheap

perhaps it's the warmer weather
that brings out the worse in
humanity today was no different

a graffiti tag more social statement than
art spells out a truth tourism kills the city
tourist go home you are not welcome here

no disguised pained reality
here economic salvation in
dollar kroner yen converted into euros

stabilizes the unstable temporarily
stealing the heart cheating the
culture erasing the meaning of home

now a white van takes
center stage and speeds
one step and two so much

                fear replaces lazy
                strides up and down
                sangria-filled eyes watching

                others in a human zoo
                growing throngs suddenly flee
                la rambla teems with bodies

observing screams cries death
on four wheels everyone
is and feels barcelona today

overwhelmed walkway crowded with flowers
beautiful barcelona covered with dead
bodies of gawkers and coffee drinkers

marchers cry out from fear and pain
the crowd's refrain – we will not be
defeated today catalonia is a part of
españa

everything is the same but different
defying calls to stay home brings
more people out into the streets

strangers weep openly together
embracing anger against tourist tempered
collective expressed pain can be beautiful

for a moment grief bridges the divide
today we are all barcelona
beautiful barcelona

There Is Such a Man

Trees bend their branches towards the Earth. Lend and
borrow wisdom for free.

There are small pockets of reality

                moving around in the
        universe.

However if you don't

                move around in the universe
        those small pockets never appear to you.

Take for instance the soul seeker who

                moves from place
        to place but never really moves his life's position.

He's the same but he thinks that he is different.

                There is such a man.
        I know him quite well.

Svalbard, Norway

*Svalbard, Norway, archipelago, is beautiful. Aurora
Borealis' stunning show, blue glacial ice sculptures
penetrating through the Arctic Ocean, midnight sun –
the northernmost year-round settlement on Earth.*

He was mauled by a polar bear – almost dead.
A swipe across his chest – likely dead.
A swipe across his throat – instantly dead.
Perhaps it was because he had more meat on him
than the rest of his tent mates – fat shamed dead.

*Untouched arctic wilderness and unique wildlife in a
rugged and fragile setting halfway between Norway
and the North Pole where there are more polar bears
than people.*

Adventurous exploration in the environment
of the largest land carnivore is not child's play –
He learned to shoot a gun two days before – trigger dead.
Chances of being attacked and killed by a polar bear are slim –
less than one hundred recorded attacks in less
than two-hundred years – twenty-one dead.

*Guaranteed to see the northern lights during the Polar
Winter or your money back. Bring warm clothes, your
camera – guns will be provided.*

Reflections On A Lived Life

Stand searching in a resurrected door that opens to the past,
present and future.
Freeing the key sewed deep in the suit pocket –
a decision must be made.

It was not an option to return to the place
where it all began
Because it burned down and buried the pain and
disappointment in the ashes left behind.

The suit is too old, too tight, too much to wear.
What else to wear? An old t-shirt, barely held together jeans,
sneakers with no laces and the tongue hanging out?
It is bitter bitter sweetness to be in this predicament.

No matter what is worn nothing can disguise the fact
something did not work out for me.
It may not be clear by looking at me
that life failed me or that I failed life.

At this point, I honestly cannot tell
who failed who. But for good measure,
and I am feeling generous,
I will say that we failed each other.

The Body Possessed

write   think   dream   act
        become   the words that meet in a dream

pass by   on the streets
        in the air   on the walls

a journey called living   taking center stage
        existing   fully   wonderfully

write   speak   think   engage
        the world   as it engages

write   speak   think   believe
        waves   toes stuck in the sand

skin on fire
        fingers twist   the wind

move   without a head
        impossible   leap   forward

leaving   only the unreasonable part
        that refuses to bend

Walking Tour in Vilnius, Lithuania

           drinkers walking tour
           through Vilnius
           cobbled stone streets
           hiking trails looming
           perch above seeing
           everything that's familiar
although it's not
sky's the limit
for smart people
who took back
generational homes when
Soviet occupation ended
           skip along paths
           things touch joy
           hopeful future seekers
           now embrace capitalism
           because the future
           is never certain
remember Russia France
streets underfoot trampled
starving soldiers memories
dead youth old
at city's gates
perished starved future

three crosses overlook
buildings river movement
wonder wander bare
our DNA coded
1905 1920 1992
always tread lightly
it's easy to
forget that freedom
can be lost
when the future
leaves no room
for the past

Mind Left to Wonder

Waking up wishing that things were clear.

                    Finding peace   solace in the
            things that are vague and intangible   make
                        cracks   in belief.
Every thought   a doubted question.

                    People don't step into life and live.
            Perhaps death could make
                    more sense   of the people in it.   Even
        rebels get tired of
being the fringe.   Stop   think   desire   understand.

                    Obsessed with the possession of
            love   ruins the mess created
                    when longing piles up.   Sense of the
        nothing   that is senselessness   in the everything
that is beautiful.

Song. Mourn.

The leaves fall from the tress.

The photo artist with the long neck, long fingers, long words
                sits embracing angels
Locked in looking out   traces of light
                seep through green canopies of forced thought
Watch
        Wobble
                Weak
Fall away shadows   leave behind naked
                death is the fire behind every kiss
Fingers strip
        Neck bent
                Words linger
A homage to life   and the hated reality of dying
                Weave together stories on paper   song of
liturgy   above   and   below

My Lover Tells Me

My lover stands on the waters edge   and tells me all of the
        things   that I don't want to know.

Something to cry out loud about
lays on the ground underfoot
falling sheets of ice make it slippery
but it is not wet

            Dreams wake up the secrets that
            are quickly forgotten when
            eyes are open and the truth
            is needed

                Wading through the rivers body
                searching beneath
                the current's twisting hands
                keep steady

Challenges await on the edge of
the cliff
it's safe
if reached a sacrifice is required

>> Controlled by the toll keeper
wailing and
gnashing
will not be avoided

>>> There is another way to get there
but it requires
something
that isn't yours to give

Failing to Write Pain on Paper

failing to write pain on paper
when i was younger living in
angst was just what it was
but now surviving it
is no longer the daily routine

it's me thriving past the dark
places that made me wet the
bed until i was 14 and made
me run into the arms of jesus
to avoid

but to find enough time to
understand the devil more clearly
the bible spells out who the devil
is he's a lot nicer than the
devils you don't know disguised

in religious clothing speech
you learn to define them when
you meet a child molester in the family
a violent domestic abuser neighbor who
killed his wife maybe himself when

you get past the need to
see the pain in black and
white it seems like you have
made it to some secret place
inside of yourself that you knew

was there but did not know
how to find it taking the
words to frame the magic of
what it means to write without
pain without past it's a freedom

that is so sweet and so
real that it makes looking back
at what you overcame difficult
it must be what an addict feels

when they finally kicked their habit
threw the monkey to the wolves

but suddenly find that they are
in a familiar place – suffocation
the relived pain is real but
it is clear that is not
where you are just a reminder

that it's waiting for you when
or if so writing about things
that light up the world and
make living better than the old
notion of it being worse sits

on my back like angel's wings
and i can hold my heart
in the palm of my hands
and see it not in that
cartoon shape but the organ thumping

veins and arteries the attachments to
the rest of me but instead
of crawling out of my skin
to save myself i embrace the
essence of me in it's physical

form writing about the world connected
to freedom to not dwell on
the ugly places is a gift
i read the newspapers listen to
the commentary know that it's bad

out here in the world and
when i attempt to write pain
on paper i have nothing to
say nothing to add that has
not already been added

of course i can put my spin on
it share my perspective on atrocities
and tragedies but others have done
it more justice and seem to
be more adept at being angry

feeling sad and fighting for change
perhaps i am numb and mistake
my ability to only write the
happy things the curiosities of trees
can i sing for the loss

of life like nina simone escape
to a foreign land like james
baldwin to write not as a
negro writer but a writer only
to return more full of rage

because nothing changed there are stories
in me poems in me words
that can be recited for worship
meetings daily mantras the evolution of
me on paper a screen reflected

back to me in completed lines or
distorted configurations of letters that take
shape in the most uncomfortable positions
free at last free at last
to write joy on paper to

have hope light the dark hours
makes it much easier to dance
with the devil than the reverse
should i fill my creative space
energy with the things that make

living difficult or rather should i
trace the silver lining to its
end so i can write my
pain and joy on the same
pages fill them with my contradictions

Acknowledgments

Where does one start, when they are acknowledging those who have contributed to goals that were not their own but nonetheless helped you realize your own?

My sisters, Gerwayne, Ernesta, Lynn and Courtney for their excitement, questions, push, belief and support of my dreams. In particular I would like to thank my twin sister. Who reminds me to call myself what I am "a writer", and who provides feedback and editing services even when I don't ask but need it.

I would like to thank Ken my mentor, friend, and book editor, for trusting me to live a full life that will fulfill my dreams. Because he plans to live vicariously through me.

My kjæreste Stig Marlon Weston who has read, critiqued, debated, listened, explored, explained, encouraged and pushed me to keep working. It is nice to share this journey with a creative and passionate person who does not require me to explain myself.

Where would one be without friends who listen and tell you
that you are the best and that they will buy your book no matter
what? There are so many friends who have just encouraged
me to go for it and who have expressed support in ways that I
am forever touched and honored.

And my dear Norwegian five; Hanne, Helle, Ingvild, Tone, and
Yngvild for opening up their world of artistic creativity through
friendship, openness and support to assist me in pursuing my
passion.

A huge thanks to Can Serrat Artist Center for accepting me
in my first residency as a writer. And to Litteraturhuset in
Oslo, Norway for allowing me space in its writer's loft.